AF059403

Rosemary Anne Mills is a writer and author but identifies herself as a storyteller who enjoys writing narrative poetry.

She was born in Cheshire, UK, but now lives in the county of Shropshire and is a 'country woman' at heart.

Whilst completing her first speculative science fiction novel for publication, she received a diagnosis of having bowel cancer. This knowledge did not stop her from writing and enjoying being a member of a local writer's group.

She wrote this narrative poetry book, under the pseudonym of 'Lady Dragon,' to separate her poetry from her speculative science fiction stories.

The aim of Rosemary's book is to give hope to all those cancer patients; reminding them that there can be life after cancer.

Cancer does not discriminate between life-forms, and she feels strongly that a cure for all cancers is vital. Meanwhile people must speak openly about fears, disappointments, financial hard-ships, and loneliness associated with cancer because these issues overshadow the healing process.

She states in her book that if her *Narrative Reflections* helps one person, her time authoring this book has been worthwhile.

Figure 1. 'Each new dawn – brings forth hope!

"When I open my eyes each and every morning and find I am not dead, I realise I am blessed to enjoy another day – whether it be a good, bad or very bad day – that is God's gift!"

This book is a dedication to my family, my medical cancer team and close friends who helped me to recover after a significant bowel cancer operation.

Lady Dragon

NARRATIVE REFLECTIONS

Book 1

AUSTIN MACAULEY PUBLISHERS™
LONDON · CAMBRIDGE · NEW YORK · SHARJAH

Copyright © Lady Dragon 2022

The right of Lady Dragon to be identified as author of this work has been asserted by the author in accordance with section 77 and 78 of the Copyright, Designs and Patents Act 1988.

All rights reserved. No part of this publication may be -reproduced, stored in a retrieval system, or transmitted in any form or by any means, electronic, mechanical, photocopying, recording, or otherwise, without the prior permission of the publishers.

Any person who commits any unauthorised act in relation to this publication may be liable to criminal prosecution and civil claims for damages.

A CIP catalogue record for this title is available from the British Library.

ISBN 9781398414594 (Paperback)
ISBN 9781398406605 (ePub e-book)

www.austinmacauley.com

First Published 2022
Austin Macauley Publishers Ltd®
1 Canada Square
Canary Wharf
London
E14 5AA

Stonehenge information:
https://wikipaedia.org/wiki/stonehenge
Photographs of Stonehenge:
https://pixabay.com/images/search/stonehenge
Music recording –William Lawes/Composer:
https://Wikipaedia.org/William Lawes
Microsoft – Photo Edits and Creating Filters.
Picture of 'Young Peasant Woman with a straw hat sitting in the Wheat' – painting by Vincent Van Gogh, courtesy of: www.vincent.van/goghgallery.org.

Special thanks to:
'New Chapter Writers.'
The group member's prompts, each month have proved most enlightening.

Table of Contents

Disclaimer	13
Why I Wrote This Book	14
Everyone Has a Special Gift	15
"Welcome"	16
Dreams and Hallucinations	17
Narrative: The Visitation	18
Poem The Visitation	22
Home At Last	28
Poem My Joyful Tears	31
Mothers Are Special	33
Life Goes On!	34
Poem The Haunting	37
Poem Celebration Time	40
Healing the Mind and Body	42
Poem The Waterfall's Prophesy	43
Friends	47
Poem Friendship	49
Poem Love	50
My Garden	54
Cancer	57
Introduction to Two More Poems	59
Poem I Am Cancer	60
Poem Cancer I Hear Your Threat	62
Cancer and Life	65

Hope	69
Poem Hope	70
Earth Angels?	71
Poem Earth Angels	74
Dreamcatcher	77
Poem Dreamcatcher	78
Poem No. 1 December's Black Moon	82
Poem No. 2 Onlookers Beware	85
Poem No.3 A Phenomenon of Universal Proportions	88
Poem A Meadow in the Spring	91
Foreword	94
Poem Home Is Where the Heart Is	95
To Honour a Friend in Heaven	99
Nature	101
Poem Time to Put the Bees to Bed	103
The Value of Interests, Hobbies and Friendships	108
Poem The Artist's Model	110
Poem A New Dawn	113
How Do You See Yourself?	116
Poem I Am a Droplet in the Ocean of Time	117
Healers	120
Recuperation Takes Time	122
Stonehenge	124
Poem Circle of Light	126
Afterword	129
"There Can Be Life After Cancer"	130
I, Say to You	131
Poetic Tribute to My Dad	133
'Happiness Ahead'	136
"Clap hands, in tribute to all cancer warriors."	137

"Cancer, must not define our identity."

Lady Dragon
Book 1

Lady Dragon

Figure 2. Author: Rosemary Anne Mills (Lady Dragon).

Disclaimer

This book reflects my own experiences, thoughts, and feelings and therefore it is not a guideline for anyone – especially those who are suffering from any form of disease or illness.

Recommend that you always inform your GP, surgeon, and oncological team before you partake in any form of alternative medicine, therapy, or practices. Complete honesty between you and your medical practitioners is essential for your good health, safety, and well-being.

This book is not a guideline for anyone who is suffering from an illness or disease of any kind.

It merely represents the author's thoughts and narrative feelings.

The author recommends that anyone who is suffering from any form of illness or disease contact their GP, consultant, oncologist, and other medically qualified persons.

Why I Wrote This Book

The aim of 'Narrative Reflections,' is to give hope to all those who are fighting cancer at present or re-building their lives after cancer because we must all remember,

"Cancer, must not define our identity."

May my story inspire others to fulfil their potential – despite illness, disease, cancer, mental health issues or any form of disability-*think-> ability**

Cancer does not discriminate between religions, cultures, beliefs, or sexual orientation – nor should we.

People who are poorly need compassion. I always loved listening to my Sunday school teacher reading '*The Good Samaritan.*' A story of compassion, from the Bible.

Please accept my humble prayer for good health and well-being.

'God grant me the Serenity
To accept the things I cannot change…
Courage to change the things I can…
and Wisdom to know the difference…' Amen.

Everyone Has a Special Gift

"You are a Warrior because you are fighting cancer."

Firstly, we must learn to love the 'new' person who stares back at us from our mirrors.

Cancer must not change– our aims, thoughts, ambitions, and our outlook on life!

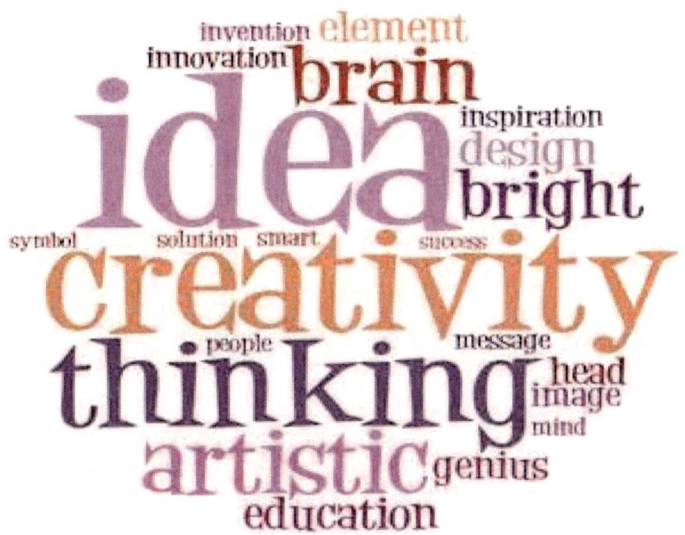

"Welcome"

The daffodil symbolises different things to different people.
    For example, it is the symbol of Wales and displayed on St David's Day – the Patron Saint for Wales.
    It is also a symbol used by 'Marie Curie.ORG.UK.' whose quote is,
'Wear your daffodil today.'

Adore- daffodils and plant daffodil bulbs all around your garden, so we can all enjoy springtime's beauty.

Dreams and Hallucinations

The following poem represents one of my more pleasant and hallucinatory experiences after my Bowel cancer operation when I was prescribed Morphine for my pain.

Did experience hallucinations – for a while-after returning home; until my bloodstream cleansed itself and my mind became clearer.

Decided to write down, my hallucinations in poetic form because I had hoped that written exercise, would help my mind to heal itself and it did.

Always adored Wild Cats, so it was of no surprise to me that wild tigers appeared as my protectors in my dreams.

People may find it wrong for me to write about drug-induced hallucinations but if my shared experience helps one person, I shall be pleased.

Narrative: The Visitation

My first tiger appeared to me in black and white, but I was not afraid; so, I said to him,
 "Hello, Tiger, how beautiful thou art."

Figure 3. My created image of my dream Tiger.

Shortly afterwards, my hallucinations appeared to me in glorious colours – often intermingled according to my state of mind.

Imagine my delight at seeing such beautiful sentient beings. Reactions must have amused my fellow companion patients in that bay of that surgical ward.

Eyes fully open, when my Tigers appeared before me and when I commented to a fellow patient,
"Love, your Tiger pillows. They are so beautiful."

With a pitiful smile, she answered,
'Rosemary! I do not have any pictures of Tigers on my cushions – let alone pillows. Are you feeling all right?'

Replied,
"Look! They are now everywhere. Their coats are in shades of gold, beige and white and they are sitting in sun-filled cornfields, and they have cubs too."

******

I created this picture, below, to portray my beautiful sentient visitors, who made themselves comfortable on my hospital bed; to protect me from harm. Well! That is how I interpreted their 'visitation' and that experience, gave me comfort and hope.

Afterword:

The black area of the Tiger picture created by me, is there to represent how close I sensed death's presence, at that given moment; whilst experiencing my hallucinatory dream.

Poem
The Visitation

Heaven's stairway appeared before my eyes.

Body and mind guided by my drifting soul.
To that heavenly, celestial plane.

My 'first-footing' paralysed, in time.

Senses'- made aware of sentient beings' presence.

Before my weary eyes- appeared,
Bengal and Snow Tigers; their footsteps everywhere.

God's sentient beings filled my mindscape, heart, and soul.

Tigers. Admittedly, my sense of reality lost.

No fear had I!
For they were my Guardians.

The male Tiger introduced me to his family, while.

Drip, drip, steady, controlled, calculated, Morphine entered my bloodstream.

Drifted-away, into that Neverland of Darkness.

"Is this death? Or is it Heaven?"

While silent tears, flowed from my eyes.

Excruciating, endless pain,
replaced by another hallucinatory dream.

'Domestic cats' I had been told to expect as visitors.

Not I! Always that person who took the wild path of life.

Drip, drip, eyelids heavy, mindscape fogged.

Reality, floated away, and my visitors returned.

Majestic Tigers everywhere,
They had decided to stay.

Floating Tigers above my head with balanced bushy tails.

Unique markings of which I had noted.

Forward, towards my neighbour's bed, they chased.

Landed with such force, I feared the Earth would shake.

Watched with glee, as Tiger cubs crawled; ready to pounce.

Upon my neighbour who seemed unaware.

Filled with dread, I said,
"Take care, before you rest upon your cushions so fair,

Beautiful Tiger cubs have settled there."

My amused fellow patient replied,
'What? There are no live Tigers upon my cushions. Are you feeling all right?"

No answer gave I, mind elsewhere.

Shivered, within those Himalayan, icy, mountain peaks.

"Hello, wait for me!"

That startled Snow Tiger mother and cubs heard my call.

Pity and empathy reflected, from their knowing eyes.

Dizzy-headed, pained and confused, I declared,

"Look! Siberian Tigers are there – over there; just behind you. Sauntering in and out of their domains."

Clapped my hands with glee, while my translucent face smiled, before I said,
"Look, listen!"

Wild cat's purring had overpowered my senses.

Lost, within my dreams and time itself.
"What a wondrous sight!"

The silent, listener was, dumbfounded.

Eyes' which wobbled, uncontrollably.
To the left, then to the right, dizzy-minded, floating visions.

Those Tigers roared,

'Fear not! For we are your guardians.'

Beautiful Tigers surged forward towards my bed.
The Tiger had left his jungle home to guard me.

Purposely, he jumped on to my bed and cleansed my face with love.

Protector purred and his tenderness entered my soul.

Eyes peering – yet!
Softly soothing my woes.

Tiger roared,
'Come forward, to greet your new friend.'

Suddenly, that Tiger's mate appeared with two cubs in-tow.

"Yes, yes, come closer. Please do."

Two miniature guardians, stripes, and all; joined the others – at my feet.

"Look, everyone, I am no longer alone," I sobbed.

With tenderness, which only a mother knows,

She grabbed each of her cubs by the back of the neck.

One by one, she placed them into my open arms.
Grateful tears trickled down my cold cheeks.

Their purring denoted their trust.

Surely a display of mutual respect?

"Mother, my toes are so cold!"

Without hesitation, she nudged her babies, and they did lay across my frozen toes.
All safe and blessed with a mother's love, was I.

With sparkling eyes – ever smiling,
She tiptoed closer over my limp and cold body.

Looked deeply into my hopeful eyes and whispered into my ear,

'We bring you, love in its purest form. Nature's gift of innocence." She purred and I smiled.

I felt warm, cosy, and safe in that believer's breast. She understood, for our minds were one,

'Faith for-ever linked to Mother Earth's sentient beings.'

The male, Tiger stood on guard while his mate fed her cubs.

Whispered in that mother's ear,
"Honoured that you visit my dreamscape world."

Mind, body, and spirit had found serenity.

Blessed and contented when I said to her,

"Thank you. You have filled my heart and soul with new-found hope."

Drip, drip, steady, controlled, calculated Morphine, entered my bloodstream.
No longer afraid for God's sentient beings were my guardians.

He, who must be 'obeyed' sent my guardian angels to me!

God's sentient beings.
My visiting Tiger companions had protected me from harm,

In my personal Equinox, dreamscape world.

***

Afterword:
"Sometimes, our subconscious knows that we do have a choice between beauty and darkness."

Home At Last

Shortly after, I returned home from the hospital, to find an unexpected gift from a dear friend.

A gift in the form of a lovely display of silk flowers and hidden within were four pairs of colourful ankle socks; to keep my toes warm.

Grateful to that kind person had taken time out of her busy day to remember me.

I immediately grabbed hold of a pen and a sheet of blank paper and drafted a poem meant to reflect my joy.

Figure 4. My lovely and colourful gift from my friend.

Here is that poem which I dedicate to my dear friend Margaret.

Poem
My Joyful Tears

Knock, knock, the Postman, had arrived.
He carried a surprise package from a thoughtful friend.
An unexpected, thoughtful, and surprising gift.

It lifted my spirits and my depression turned into delight.
Once unpacked, tears of joy. Fell softly down my pale cheeks.

"Behold! Creative rainbow roses hand-made from silk."

Lavender tissue paper completed that rainbow bouquet.

Chosen with care and sent with empathy.

"Oh! My favourite colours!"

A thoughtful gift sent by a selfless and sensitive friend.

Remembered, saying to that friend,
'How cold my feet are.'

And she had listened well.

For hidden amongst the pink, oyster and peach, white roses,
and silk ribbons.

Warm, pink, sky blue and navy-striped bed socks disguised –
as flowers.

A bouquet most rare because of the thoughtfulness she had enclosed in there.

Sweet, soft water seeped from my tired eyes.

Spark of hope emerged – from deep within my soul.

My, friend's kindness, had filled my heart with joy.

Tears of emotion exploded!

Knowing one special and unique friend.

Had taken precious time out of her busy day.
To choose a gift for her poorly friend.

Mum was right when she said to me,

'We cannot choose our family, but we can choose our friends.

'Remember,
'Some friends are bronze, for they are strong.

'Other friends are silver because they shine.

'Special friends – who are there for you when others flee –

'Are the golden, priceless ones; for their hearts are pure and full of love!'

Written: 07-04-2018.

******

Mothers Are Special

Here is a fourth-generation photograph of four incredibly special mothers - to me.

Figure 5. Grandmother, mother, sister, niece, and great nephew Andrew – four generations in the same family. Photographed by Nantwich Chronicle's photographer – our own copy. *Our families are held-fast by women of substance, but they are not immune to cancer. *

Life Goes On!

Hallucinations continued for weeks, after I had returned home, due to an infection around my navel wound – despite my prescriptive antibiotics.

As stated earlier, the Morphine administered into my bloodstream – whilst in hospital resulted in pleasant hallucinations where Tigers visited me in my dreams.

Unfortunately, those sweet dreams turned into nightmares and during those weeks my sleep pattern was disturbing, and I slept within my bedroom, with the electric lights on.
 Ghoulish and evil spirits were my companions. It was a short but unpleasant experience which I would not wish on anyone.

Time heals everything – so, they say!

As my infection healed – due to the wonderful nursing care I received from our district nurses, my body cleansed itself and the nightmares ceased – Hallelujah!
***
Almost, a year later, I received a writing prompt whilst attending my local writer's meeting. The prompt, linked to a piece of classical music. When I listened to that piece of music my subconscious awoke, and the following poem describes that specific moment.

I present to you, my poem titled:

        'The Haunting.'

The Haunting.

The scene:

Imagine, a grief-stricken woman, sitting on a small, wooden chair in a dark and sparsely furnished room. Beside her, a small table; where a single-lit candle is her only solace and protection for the spirits which surround her."

Poem
The Haunting

Haunting, disturbing, deathly shadows.
Flickering candlelight, ghostly presence.
Melodious melancholy.

Death mocks silent tears.
Emotions set free.
Emotional disharmony.

Flickering candlelight, visiting spirits.
Wavering before her and the widow- lost in sorrow.
Melodious melancholy.

Mournful pain, heartfelt lament.
Her solemn, grieving dignity.

"Sorrow was, as sadness is,
"Melodious melancholy."

Written: 05-06-2019.

    Afterword: The music I listened to was by William Lawes *'She Weepeth sore in the night.'*

To follow, is an additional poem which I wrote in honour of that great Composer: William Lawes (1625–50).

Poem
Celebration Time

Composer's Fantasia for his king.
The welcoming fanfare begins.
Gentle, serene melody.
Instrumental complexity.

Who would have thought this youthful cavalier?

Mindful of his royal responsibilities,
Composed such a delightful style.
Virtuoso's modern mind.

Composer's Fantasia for his king.
Brought forth such a time-full score.

Composition filled with instrumental diversity.
A creative virtuoso, with an organised mind.

The king's composer who died so young.
Both cavalier and composer combined.

A musician. The performer of his day – so revered!
Immortal, fantasia for his king.

******

Figure 6. Artist's impression of William Lawes – Wikipedia.

Healing the Mind and Body

"With time, hope, love and good friends, one's body and mind can heal."

As my body healed, I returned to writing more joyful poems and continued the writing of new stories.

Here, is one that I enjoyed writing for it inspired me to write a new Speculative Science Fiction Novel.

If you enjoy stories based upon legends and the mysterious aura of waterfalls this next poem may be one for you to enjoy.

The poem titled: The Waterfall's Prophesy.

Figure 7. My own photograph.

Poem
The Waterfall's Prophesy

Snow-capped mountains gave way to spring's sunshine glow.

White water began to move freely, gained momentum, as it flowed down stream.

Meltwater crashed furiously powered by nature's haste.
Not a place where mortal man belongs, for he is not part of the equation.

There is no way to stop this icy journey.
White water's fury continued with intent.

Through polished and treacherous rocks and boulders.
Sculptured by winter's demise, as spring's time was in place.

Where moss and fauna could not grasp or take hold.
Over frozen tundra, the icesheet gained momentum.

Down, down, towards the Lake.
Where God rules the natural state.

At lightning speed, Brightwater's delight approached the cliff's edge.
No time to stop and pause.

Time is ripe with urgency.
Nature demanded her legacy as the natural lake was in sight.

Majestically, the mystique 'Lady of The Lake' waited patiently.

Yet! Anxious for the renewal of her life's mythology.
For her dark, deep grave – is hers alone.

Not a place where mortal man belongs.
For he is not part of the equation.

The sacrificial holy water was committed to its fate.
It tumbled, crashed thunderously, o'er the water's edge.

Accepted nature's destiny, it fulfilled its promises – made in times of old.

To a lady resolute in league with Merlin's sorcery.
No place where mortal man belongs unless called to deliver!

Mystical, foretold destinies when magic plied nature's alchemy.

Forward, the thunderous foaming white water surged.

Down, down, it gathered speed for time was of the essence.
Nature rules as nature should!

Only chosen birds passed through, those clouds of mist which formed.
To nest within the boulder's dark and dry crevices.

Safe from regal predators – who fly on high
God's sentient beings – nature doth protect.

A rainbow crowned that waterfall, denoted its prophesy.
Nature rules, as nature should, majestic in simplicity.

No place where mortal man belongs unless his divine destiny.

The white waters called out,
'Nearly there.'

Froth embedded boulders of ancient times,
Bordered the lady of the lake's abode.

Aquatic lifeforms enjoyed that oxygenated water.
Renewed their lake's immortality,
when they filled their gills and drew breath.

Foaming water, muffled, mingled, and meandered around embedded boulders.
Never fearful of those undercurrents and hidden within that deep and sleepless bed.

Yet! Respectful of nature's authority as a natural entity.
A place where no mortal man belongs.

Nature's everlasting consistency, gave life to all and may all praise, the epitaph of alchemy; or is it so?

For mankind's folklore and mythology brought forth energy and creativity.

Humankind must walk in harmony; with God's gift he gave to thee!

'Fear not, death!'

For the lady of the lake waits patiently still- for Merlin to re-appear.
Written: 26-07-2019

***

Afterword:

"As a child I enjoyed reading mythical stories of King Arthur and the Magician or Sorcerer -Merlin.

Is there an under-world, where magic reigns?

I do not know.

A world without magic would be boring.

Along with our sense of curiosity and imagination, lives enriched by magic, mythology, folklore, and literature.

Friends

One appreciates those friends, who support us when we are poorly.

Authored a short poem for special friends, who were there for me, when I needed them most.

Sometimes, it is not always the friends which we have known the longest but those friends who step forward for us.

Everyone needs a friend to confide in, share our fears with and understand our need to rebuild our confidence after trauma, illness, or family crisis.

No two people are alike and likewise, no two friends are either.

Friendship is a 'two-way' affair for caring, sharing and nurturing which is based on trust. For without trust – there is nothing!

A lot of my 'friends' enjoy the love and companionship of their beloved pets – as I do.
To follow is my poem titled: ***Friendship.***

"Friendship comes forth in many guises."

Figure 8. Spring's first primroses for my friends.

Poem
Friendship

What is life without friendship?
How boring life would be!

Strangers come into our lives for a reason.
Friends listen, advise, cheer, cry and laugh with us.

Friends never judge but accept us – unconditionally.
You – yes, you are my friend, despite the miles that divide us.

We share 'mutual friends' that are true, loyal, and sincere.
We share values and the love of nature, animals, and life itself.

Our beloved dogs are surely friends too.
For they not only enrich our lives but our friendships too,
"Thank you," for being our friend.

Poem
Love

Firstly said, one -by - one, 'I love you.'
In unison, two said, 'I love you too.'
Now united by a love most true.
So, love is all, love is you.

Love-endeavoured, by time.
Love's adaption from an individual's mind.
Love combines soul mates,
Which is thy other self.
Love is all, love is you.

Love is children, God's blessing to you.
Love, which has passed the test of time,
Brings forth family bonding time.
Love is all, love is you.

Love is courage, trust, loyalty, and respect.
Love endeavours with fortitude.
Love conquers, heals, and grows.
Love is pure and unquestioning.
Love is all, love is you.

Love is a bond unbounded.
Love needs to breathe.
Love is hope for all humanity.
Love is all, love is you.

Written: 26-12-2018.

***

Afterword:
"Wrote this poem for my close family members, who have always been there for me and never let me down but encouraged, trusted me; thus, allowing us to be 'best friends forever.'

'How do we define Love?

Sometimes, the purest way to show your love is to keep it simple.

A single red rose speaks volumes, whereas flowers in mass can result in that love token -lost in commercialism.

It is not necessary to spend enormous amounts of money on trendy gifts – to show your love.

My, family have never known financial wealth, but we are indeed, enriched with love.

Would rather receive a posy of hand-picked wildflowers from a child than an expensive bouquet from a shop!

Surely, the thought which has gone into that 'posy.' Is a simple gift of love, everlasting joy, and happiness.

Remember:

Those, who take time out of their day, to check you are all right, for they are priceless.

We each make our own heaven or hell on this Planet Earth.

'Seize the day' – enjoy it.

Whether a day be a good or difficult – remember, life is precious and not promised.

My Garden

My garden is my sanctuary, for it gives me joy – no matter which season we are in.

I have always, managed to forget my troubles, renew my faith, and gain strength from being in my garden.

Taught as a child, that 'we come into this world with nothing and that is how we leave it'-such a lesson learned so early in life; tends to stay with you throughout adulthood.

Therefore, my garden, is God's Garden and as his gardener, I tend, tidy, plant and sit happily within the garden itself.

"In the summertime, my garden is where I do my creative writing- with my ScottieFox chow for company and inspiration."

Picture below:

My outside, summertime writing desk- where only the melodious sounds of wild birds interrupt my thoughts.
 "Pen, blank sheets of paper and sun."

As a 'welcome' to visitors to my home I planted roses close to my home's entrance door.
Red roses – for love.
Yellow roses – for friendship

Cancer

Cancer is a subject which too many people are afraid to speak openly about – not I!

Sometimes, people change their attitude towards cancer patients – they think they will 'catch it,' silly presumption but it did happen to me,

"Hey! Still the same lovable person I was before cancer invaded my body."

***

"The open discussion about cancer must continue."

Futuristic thoughts:

It is a blessing that we cannot predict the future, although there are those out there who pretend to be able to do so.

One of the most critical issues that the World Health Organisation and world governments, is for them all to learn to work together, to find a cure for cancer.

All sentient beings on this Planet Earth are prone to cancer. Cancer does not discriminate!

Cancer has its eye upon us all, so we must work together to find a solution.

Introduction to Two More Poems

Writer, who found herself diagnosed as having Bowel cancer, by my surgeon's cancer teams and that knowledge changed my whole outlook on life.

Therefore, I decided to write two poems with a 'cancer' theme.

Decided to keep the two poems simple, with no frills or excess sentimentality.

The first poem states cancer's aim.

The second poem is from a cancer sufferer's point of view – mine but maybe – just maybe – you, the reader- may empathise with its message and tone.

Aimed, to keep my two poems clear-cut – hopefully, the reader will relate to the urgency for scientists, to find a cure for all cancers!

All life-forms are prone to one form or another of cancer.

Poem
I Am Cancer

Cancer am I!
Not prejudicial – no! Not I.

Here when the universe formed.
Shall be here, till the end of time.

Unless humanity takes up the fight and
Scientists find a cure – before I mutate!

All sentient beings are on my list to kill.
Not prejudicial – no, not I.

Transmutations despite genetic complexities.
Strength lies in, mankind's complacency.

If scientists cannot find a cure, before I mutate?
Shall be here, until the end of time.

***

Foreword:

Dedicate this poem to my dear brother, Robert James Mills.

For Robert-known to his friends and family, simply as, 'Bob' has 'fought the good fight' against cancer for over twelve years thus far.

And, for those – who are in the same 'cancer club.'

Poem
Cancer I Hear Your Threat

Cancer, I hear your threat.
Strong-willed am I, and ready to fight.

What is that you say,
'Cannot win?'

Tis, you -Cancer that should tremble in fear – not I!

I, with the rest of humanity, pledge our union,
To eradicate your ambitious folly.

Hidden within our genetic code, lies the answer.
Scientists shall discover your weakness and defeat you.

Human. Human, am I.
Humans are no longer complacent.

We fight 'fire with fire.'
Cancer, listen and learn,

"Your reign on Planet Earth is about to end.
"It is you that should tremble in fear – not I."

******

Afterword: Let us all 'fight the good fight with all our might.'
We must defeat cancer in all its forms.
This burden does not and should not, depend upon scientists alone because we must all take better care of our health.
The unification of the human spirit can help us all to survive against all the odds.

Surely, our 'loved ones and our future children expect no less from us but to continue forward- as 'Cancer Warriors.'

Figure 9. Good health to you all.

Cancer and Life

Humankind is one big family, despite our diversity.
A family who must work together to fight cancer with all its complexities.

"Remember, it is essential to plan for the future but more important, to enjoy each and every single day; whether it be a good or bad-day."

Life is always worth fighting for; so, please- never give up on life until it gives up on you!

Life goes on and while we are alive, we must all appreciate and concentrate upon what we can do, rather than what we cannot do.

Follow that dream, complete that task, project, or quest- which makes your life-truly fulfilled.

Each of us are unique and deserve a good-quality life. Do not let cancer deny you opportunities, which life may offer you.

Time is the one element in life we cannot control or retrieve. Therefore, make your allocated time on Mother Earth worthwhile and happiness will be yours.

In order, to heal physically and mentally we need to allow ourselves the necessary time to recuperate before we can go forward.

Eat well, rest when needed, get out into the fresh air whenever possible and welcome friends and family who love and care for you.

Understand fully there are those people, who cannot do these things mentioned for themselves! For, I nursed both my parents for over twelve years and during that time – their quality of life, depended upon the quality nursing care- which I bestowed on them.

Sometimes, it is not the length of life which matters but the quality and depth while living.

The greatest act of love to bestow upon the dying, is to 'be there for them' at the end.

Lost count, of the number of times I stayed behind after my nursing shift ended - just to hold a dying patient's hand. Such acts of compassion, cost only our 'time' and because I understood that lonely, frightened patient - was 'afraid of death'-I have no regrets!

Let us not become too morbid, for life is precious and despite those 'bad days' there will be good ones for sure. The latter -will give you strength to carry-on.

The beauty of life comes from our inability to foretell the future.

Wonderful, exciting, and delightful surprises are yet to happen. Such as, a new grandchild born. This 'happening' gave my own mother a new lease of life, after she held her son's grandchild's tiny fingers within her hand for the first time.

Cancer must not break the human spirit because we are more than 'cancer patients.' We are resilient, strong willed, inventive, creative, adaptable, and unique.

Nature is a strange and unpredictable phenomenon, and it can play its part in both human and an animal's recovery from cancer.

There will be days when we are despondent because the weather is awful and venturing out may not be possible.

On the other hand, when the sun shines, the 'feel good factor' lifts our spirits.

Sunny days' and 'good days' need to be harvested within our memory banks. For we can, 'fall-back' on good memories to sustain us through those 'unbelievably - bad days.'

When you are caring for a loved-one, you freely-give T.L.C (Tender Loving Care). From that 'bonding'-both of you gain joy, happiness, and strength.

Finally, may I add that it is better to die in the arms of someone who cares and loves you, than in the company of strangers.

This applies to all creatures on Mother Earth. For when an old dog or a companion pet has given a lifetime of trust and love to its human, the least that sentient being deserves is having someone there who cares, when they cross that 'Rainbow Bridge' into heaven.

Compassion is the greatest gift we must show towards one another.

Hope

While there is hope for life – hang on to that fact.

Have faith in: Yourself, tune-into your inner strength. and willpower.
.
You may still be able to achieve your lifegoals.

And remember:
Self-empowerment will help you to overcome life's trails and in doing so, you may pleasantly surprise yourself.

Hope

Combine faith and hope, and a joyful spirit to enrich your life- despite ill health, social injustices, monetary problems, and personal heartaches.
When the restrictions of 'old age creeps-in'- without warning or a disability, thrusts itself upon you; Hope can bring you solace and a sense of well-being.

'Hope' was the last spirit to leave Pandora's box and therefore God's last gift to all.

The Knot Prayer
- Author Unknown -

Dear God,

Please untie the knots that are in my mind, my heart, and my life.

Remove the have nots, cannots, and the do nots.

Erase the will nots, may nots, might nots that may find a home in my heart.

Release me from the could nots, would nots, and should nots that obstruct my life.

And most of all, dear God, I ask that you remove from my mind, my heart, and my life all of the "am nots" that I have allowed to hold me back. Especially the thought that I am not good enough.

Amen

Encouragement from 95.1 SHINE-FM

Poem
Hope

Hope is all I have.

It is your friend and mine.

What an empty, and sad world, it would be -without hope!

No dreams envisaged, for future generations.

Hope is my gift to you.

Take it now and welcome it into your heart.

Earth Angels?

There are Earth Angels, living amongst us on Mother Earth, in the appearance of both human, and Sentient Beings.

Earth angels are the ones who go out of their way to help others and the human ones, wear a genuine smile when they listen to your woes.

There are 'animal angels' amongst us who show compassion for the plight of all sentient beings.

There are earth angels who ask no reward for helping others.

Friends' who we may never have met in person due to Facebook and other internet, can be our earth angels.

Friends' 'message' us regularly- just to check if we are all right. They too are earth angels.

Family members who take time out of their day to visit, shop for us and stay connected are, earth angels.

Our surgeons, nurses, oncologists, and other medical teams give us hope or the 'truth;' they are earth angels.

Groups of people who link up worldwide to rescue animals and work together to 'Save our planet' are earth angels.
Our surgeons, nurses, oncologists, and all medical teams- give us hope, by helping us 'come to terms' with our illnesses,

cancers and problems. Therefore, they are all priceless 'Earth Angels.'

These professional medical services have been under great personal and professional pressure during this Covid19 Pandemic. Yet, their teamwork and dedication have enabled us all to re-gain faith in our fellow men.

This COVID19 Pandemic is not over, and we shall never feel truly safe because the virus's mutations and variants' spread across the world. So, we depend too upon Scientists of the world, to find a speedy, and safe vaccination for us all. Therefore, they too are 'Earth Angels.'

We are now living within a changed world. Covid19 took the world into chaos but mankind's ability to adapt -gives us all hope, for a better future.

Meanwhile, there are people still in 'self-isolation'-who still depend upon 'essential workers. People- who have continued working throughout the Covid19Pandemic; keeping goods, supplies and our service industries going- surely, they are 'Earth Angels' too.

You must understand that there are those earth angels who do 'virtuous deeds' anonymously, because they are compassionate and 'seek no reward'.

Introduction to my next poem:

In honour of all earth angels, I authored this poem titled: 'Earth Angels.'

Poem
Earth Angels

Empathic, consciousness.
Earth Angels,
Are those who 'shine.'

Earthbound, angels.
Compassionate, dedicated.
Those who wear an aura of sincerity.

Professionalism, self-sacrificial souls.
Preservers of all life forms.
Truth Sayers.

Earth angels,
Emit confidence, encouragement, and hope.
Resolute, committed to do honourable deeds.

Earth Angels lead us into,
Sacred paths where minds can heal,
Givers of love and sincerity.

Life is sacred to earth angels.
They portray empathic consciousness,
Vocational healers and rescuers.

Earth Angels,
Truth Sayers.
Empaths who aim to heal our souls.

Earth Angels, amongst us on Mother Earth,
 not all are human.

Respect, thankfulness, and admiration,
Have I, for earth angels.
For they chose -their path in life.

Figure 10 Gifted Dreamcatcher: from an American friend.

When it arrived, my beloved, rescued Kathy chow, was having regular nightmares. I therefore hung that dreamcatcher over her bed; until her bad memories - based on past experiences disappeared.

Dreamcatcher

There are those people on planet Earth who use their talents to help us regain our sense of 'well-being.'

A good friend of mine knew that I was experiencing bad dreams and nightmares after losing my beautiful white GSD, called Hollydolly.

My lovely girl had waited patiently for me to return home from hospital and shortly after we were re-united, she died in my arms.

"Beside myself, with grief."

Knowing my sorrow, my dear friend, Cindy, commissioned the making of a special 'dreamcatcher' for me. Cindy knew that I empathised with American Indian beliefs.

Therefore, I was pleased when I unexpectedly received the gift of a custom-made Dreamcatcher from my friend Cindy.

The dreamcatcher-given an American Indian blessing, to keep me safe from nightmares in that dreamscape world of mine.

Delighted to have received such a thoughtful gift, I authored a poem titled: 'Dreamcatcher.'

Poem
Dreamcatcher

Dreamcatcher,
Welcome to this believer's abode.
Catch my negative dreams,
Bring forth happy positive memories,
Yet to happen.

My native American dreamcatcher!
Folklore denotes your beneficial powers,
While my heart grieves for my Holly Dolly.
Your presence unites us harmoniously.

My negative thoughts caught in its spider's web and destroyed at sunrise.

While my positive dreams drift down and down,
Through those brightly coloured feathers,
Into my memory bank.

The 'hoop' representing Mother Earth,
Doth spin freely.

A silver paw to remind me of my sweet angel. For Holly Dolly is in heaven and my heart doth grieve so!

A dear empathic friend sent this gift of compassion.
Created, by her friend who installed its' blessing.

Now my dreamscape world is harmonious, pleasant, and joyful once more.

Who would have thought that such a gift?

Would bring forth peace and harmony.
Why? The dreamcatcher maker and my dear, friend,
"Thank you, Cindy."

***

Foreword, to three special poems:

When people are fighting any form of illness, we are grateful- just to be alive to enjoy the changing seasons, which can bring us joy and happiness.

Prefer to call our planet 'Mother Earth,' because our planet earth must be respected- as all mothers should be.

Our planet's resources are now highly polluted, but as yet-not beyond redemption. Sentient beings are becoming sick and die because of mankind's selfish polluting practices and greed.

Mother Earth's future is in peril, which has left our people without hope.

Solace can be found-from nature's ever-evolving beauty and as more scientific facts emerge concerning our planet and the Cosmos; the more there is to learn.

Therefore, as a Science Fiction writer, I am interested in all strange phenomenon which occurs from time to time.

Therefore, I enjoy observing all strange and wonderous phases of our nearest Moon, especially when it waxes and wanes. Most exciting is when our Moon experiences an eclipse.

To follow are three poems, written in narrative form-to celebrate 'December's Black Moon' – 26-12-2018.

The first poem titled: 'December's Black Moon.'

The second poem titled: 'Onlookers Beware.'

The third poem titled: 'A Phenomenon of Universal Proportions.'

Poem No. 1
December's Black Moon

Figure 11. My Photograph.

Black Moon's eerie vista awaits its onlookers.

Inspiring, possessing and mesmerising with its hypnotic dominance.

Nature silent.
Ghostly shadows.
An evolving celestial transformation.

Black Moon's wondrous sight,
Leaves its onlookers transfixed momentarily.

Memory boxes unfolded.
Click, click, they aim to capture its image.

Underfoot is crisp and white,
For Jack Frost has danced about.

Pure oxygen the onlooker's breath in,
With heads light and disorientated.

They tremor within this eerie scene,
Almost trapped in a moonlight trance.

Black Moon's time is short and rare,
It foresees man's time on earth as fleeting.

Inspiring, possessing and mesmerising with its hypnotic dominance.
Humankind monitors Black Moon's rare celestial appearance.

Nature, silent.
Ghostly shadows.
An evolving celestial transformation.

Black Moon's time is short and rare,
It foresees man's time on earth as fleeting.

Poem No. 2
Onlookers Beware

Figure 12. My Photograph.

With patience it yields to mankind's vanity.

Black Moon's eerie glow questioned,
'What are these onlookers?'

Inspiring, possessing and mesmerising with its hypnotic stare.
Nature silent; frozen in time.

Black Moon hidden by winter's sinister naked branches.
A unique phase of Earth's closest planet.

It looks down from that winter sky.
A celestial moon in mourning?

Onlookers beware!
Is a reminder of mankind's insignificance
A magnitude beyond man's reasoning.

Black Moon's eerie and transforming glow,
Shone on the darkest of nights.

Look! How its absorption of space and light.
Is captured! Flash, flash, flash… flash.

December Black Moon paused and asked,
'Why are they here? They pay no part in my existence!'

Black Moon's light absorption now complete within that winter's night.

Its last farewell seen by all,
Within that frosty winter's night.

Black Moon's last thoughtful smile,
Was beyond mankind's comprehension.
Onlookers beware!

***

Poem No.3
A Phenomenon of Universal Proportions

Figure 13. My Photograph.

A cosmic reminder of man's insignificance.

Is Cosmogony beyond man's reasoning?

Black Moon's decisive moment has passed,
As its farewell. Left its onlookers spellbound.

Yet, Black Moon's return is inevitable.
Can humanity be so self-assured?

God, said,
'Let there be light.'

Lest December Black Moon be a celestial warning?

Preserve the peace and harmony upon this insignificant Planet Earth.

Black Moon is a phenomenon of universal proportions.
Whereas mankind's inquisitive thirst for knowledge, is yet to unfold.

A phenomenon of universal proportions.
Black Moon has bid Planet Earth 'farewell.'

***

Foreword:
We must not forget that cancer attacks all living creatures and my beautiful Hollydolly was one such victim.

Poem
A Meadow in the Spring

That spring the meadow sat within its wavering seas of gold and green.

Holly Dolly stood within her golden oceanic plankton – free spirited.

Marigolds and buttercups framed her beauty, that once was, but now departed.

She was a light enclosed by nature's flora and fauna.
Golden enchantments harmonised with tones of green.
Depicted nature's rebirth!

Emotions from that blissful sight,
Filled my senses with joy.

She stood so proud, this rose did weep,
For even love's shrouded tears.
Nature's warning sign of what was yet to happen.

Sweet sorrow is our reward,
When our memory doth reflect.

I did not foresee within that golden sea of green- nature's warning.

Sadness is grounding!

Mingled harmony was a joyful surprise,
Within that golden sea.

A memory of happier times when my Holly Dolly stood robust and free.
For there she played with her beloved companions.

Twas there she dreamt her dreams,
Chased wild rabbits, birds, and bees.
A contented sentient being of, my lament.

Now! Our beautiful white wolf doth dance with the breeze,
Unrestricted for all eternity in Heaven.

***

"R.I.P. Sweet Holly Dolly, we are not restricted to one dimension nor is our love! We shall meet again – wait for me at those golden gates of heaven."

***

Foreword

Both humans and sentient beings have their own notion of 'home.'

Home is where one feels safe, comfortable, and loved.

I daresay, a sentiment wished for by all God's sentient beings.

When I Stepped-back, I understand exactly why, I had chosen to write in a specific place in my own home; then how it made me feel but from the view of my other self!

That introspect self-analysis resulted in a narrative poem, written from an onlooker's point of view.

    The poem titled:
    'Home Is Where the heart Is.'

    Simply, an insight of my indoor-writing domain and why that room suits my persona.

Poem
Home Is Where the Heart Is

She sits within a colour scheme that denoted her love of richness. Money is not the motivation nor opulent fantasy.

Her love of vibrant colours around the room,
Denotes warmth, comfort, joy, and light.

Grounded by that homely and subdued vista,
Purple is her favourite colour,
'Bishop's Purple,' she announced to her visiting friends.
Who stood startled by her daring and artistic palette?

Yet! There, stood her family relaxed within its welcoming ambiance.

"Be fearless with your creativeness, each of us must choose our own 'path to enlightenment'," she advised.

She, who is a writer, had decided long ago,
To write word after word – till it made sense!

So, she wrote where her dogs and family,
Gathered in love and harmony.

Her creative spirit and warm heart enriched by that vibrant colour scheme.

The place where this storyteller's mind,
Came alive.

Where fairy lights add magic to the scene.
Creativity born from her wondering mindscape.

Fantasia, other beings once hidden, now step forth from behind those magical pixie's lights.
"To write creatively, one must first choose your space; where magic is welcomed."

Her desk – her domain!
An open gateway to,
'What ifs,'
Where Speculative Science Fiction breathes.

So, this writer's chosen abode,
Is a friendly, welcoming, inspiring, and creative,
Place to be.

She welcomes inspiration and visitors there,
Humans, sentient beings and spirits from other domains and dimensions.

Storytellers must explore futuristic realms,
Seeking out the essence of her characters.

Her dancing letters form words.
Word after word, sentences for a story.
So, she practices the art of epistolary!

A storyteller who travels through dimensions, time, and space.
Sometimes poetic narrative fills her senses.
Born out of warm colours – her domain!

Emotions triggered that are intangible.
Light's reflections, colour spectrum,
A mind in constant transit.

Imagination, that is hers alone,
When she journeys through time and space,
But home is where the heart is!

To Honour a Friend in Heaven

Member of Facebook and joined in 2012 and decided to write and publish regular posts on my Page titled: 'LETTER FROM ENGLAND.'

Notion to write regularly in that way, enabled me, to stay connected with friends and relatives who live outside the United Kingdom.

The 'pen-name' of 'NINA WOODY' in memory of a dear friend 'Nina' who died of cancer.

It was on one of those predicted 'bad days' when I wrote the statement below and posted it on the 'cover' of my Facebook page: "Sometimes it is essential to find that quietness from within ourselves in order to cope with all the upsets, stress and heartache which life can thrust upon us." – NINA WOODY.

Tribute, to my dear friend, Nina, who died after fighting a short battle with cancer.

Nina was Russian born, married, and moved to the UK with her husband and first-born child. We met at a local college in Cheshire as adults and became friends immediately.

Nina's character was strong, and she possessed a lively, intelligent, and inquiring mind with an unpredictable but enchanting personality which gained her hundreds of faithful and adoring friends.

Nina's heart was warm, compassionate, open-minded, and non-discriminatory and those are the qualities which both inspired her family and friends.

She was also born with an artistic gift and studied at university where she gained her Degree in Art.

"The world needs more people like Nina- who are gifted, creative, hardworking, of generous spirit, non-discriminatory and compassionate."

Nature

Nature never fails to give me strength, delight my senses and install hope for the future.

Relatives and close friends, know that one of my greatest joys in life, was when I became a beekeeper.
"Pollinators are the most precious commodity available to mankind."

Ecologists and eco-friendly scientists are doing their best to combat diseases that have already placed bees'- on the 'Endangered Species list.'

Everyone on Mother Earth must surely have realised by now that when all the Pollinators disappear so shall the food supply which we all rely upon to survive.

Whenever I find any pollinator exhausted, I take them inside and feed them either sugar syrup or honey – whatever is in my cupboard at that given time. Then they have a second life chance!

Poem
Time to Put the Bees to Bed

'A picture of my Apiary – in the early morning mist -after they have been 'Put to Bed' for the winter.'

Poem:

Seasons denote 'time' for honeybees!

Domesticated by man, defined by nature.
Conditioned by their psychological environment.

Untamed, wild, free spirits.
They accept our homage as beekeepers.

Each colony, synchronised,
Order maintained by their dominant queen.

Yet, singularly linked to the element of time.
They accept the concept of nature's rule.

Time spent foraging – an industrious life span.
Time is of the essence, for their seasons are short.

Time is their motivator!
Their biological clocks accept the coming of winter.

Throughout spring and summertime, they forage.
Collecting nectar for each communal store.

Across meadows, woods, and fields – they fly with haste.

Foragers 'wiggle dance' with bottoms high,
To disclose geographical locations for their fellow worker bees.

Days shorten, and mechanical clocks go forward.
Nature's creatures prepare their winter bed.

While these cooperative communities wait patiently, for returning workers,
Sentries guard the hives from invading foes.

Autumn is a sensitive time with pollen in short supply.
The beekeeper's homage, presented.

Beekeepers provide winter food of sugar syrup.
For time is short and the bees cannot wait.

The beekeeper's husbandry linked to cleanliness.
Honeycombs cleansed in haste.

"Inspect your Apiary's hives, dear beekeepers. Leave them clean from within but hurry, lest Jack Frost doth get in!"

Domesticated by man, defined by nature,
Honeybees are man's link to Mother Earth.

A matriarchal zone where time, space, and pollinators,
Complete nature's fragile allegory,

Tis the time. Beekeepers' feed each queen's colony in gratitude!

This maintains the equilibrium between
Humankind and nature.

Beekeepers having relocated summer's bounty pay their dues to their buzzing friends.

Nature's honey replaced by a never-ending supply of sugar syrup,
To see them through those winter blizzards.

Seasons denote 'time' for honeybees.
Time is of the essence.

"Apiaries firmly grounded,
"Ready for frosts and snowy blizzards."

Mousetraps secured to each hive's front door.
All bees gather; for they are their own winter blanket-deep inside their hives.

Finally, all hives tightly shut.
Time to put the bees to bed.

***

Yet before the beekeeper turns away, there is one last task to perform, with a gentle voice,
"Goodnight, sweet friends. Your beekeeper shall watch over you when Jack Frost is here; until spring's flowers doth open wide and warmer foraging times. Goodnight!"

Figure 14. "Beekeeper."

The Value of Interests, Hobbies and Friendships

There are so many diversional and pleasurable recreations which can bring us joy such as, music, television, clubs, and last -but not least, visiting friends.

It is a well-known fact that everyone needs to interact with people from time to time and make new friends, pursue new hobbies, which enrich our social lives and improves our sense of well-being.

Everyone must find their own 'tribe' of friends and joining a club or group where like-minded people go is a positive way to forget one's woes while enjoying the company of others.

As a member of a local writer's group, I find it mentally stimulating and challenging to interact with writers from different genres. One 'prompt' given, related to a painting by Vincent Van Gogh.

Authored a poem which related to the artist's model herself and wrote it from the model's point of view; rather than the artwork itself.

How would I feel -if I were she, who sat still for hours on end, while Vincent Van Gough captured my image in oils, on his canvas?

'Young Peasant Woman with a Straw hat sitting in the Wheat' painting by Vincent Van Gogh (A part-copy of that famous painting).

This next poem is in a simplistic, narrative form, for this is the style or format I prefer-when writing poetry. When you read this poem may the poem be inspiring you to draft a poem or story of your own.

The poem titled: The Artist's Model.

Poem
The Artist's Model

Aloof! I patiently sit within a sea of gold.
Compliant for this artist's gaze.

Know, your thoughts, as you understand mine,
'Young, yet old!' Read his mind!

Deeply tanned and flushed from my daily labour.
While Vincent's face obscured, by canvas and easel.

Proud, yet shyly, I hope that he,
May capture my life's story for all eternity

Tired eyes look elsewhere, conscious of my pinafore.
'Correct attire,' but my shyness suited- his fleeting glare.

Now his is oblivious to my peasant status.
Vincent's sunny palette- brought forth joy to my spirit.

No time for conversation, the artiste encased within creativity.
Will, humanity eventually empathise with my plight?

For I am young – not old and wear my yellow bonnet with pride,
Its blue ribbons denote my youthful sensuality.

Gratified; my deep-blue embroidered dress pleases him!
Chosen for practicality it protects me from the sun's piercing rays.

I fear not! Soon my life's story captured and resilient from time's fragility.
Within our shared love of summer's sea of gold.

He has chosen me above all others.
For his artistic creativity.

So, I sit compliant despite his artistic and assuming stare!

My yellow straw hat, worn to compliment my deep-blue dress,
It pleases this artist's spectrum – such a colourful palette.

***

"That 'Young Peasant Woman with Straw hat Sitting in the wheat.'"

"Aloof! Sitting, within a sea of gold."

Poem
A New Dawn

Figure 15. Sleep is over-rated when a new dawn is born.

Aching limbs,
Rest no longer.

Twilight zone,
Brain scrambled,
Body limp.

Curtains drawn.
Faint moon,
Shadowing trees.

Open window.
Senses soar.
Early morning chorus.

Body tingles.
Melodious bird songs,
Food for the soul.

Sun dispersed that moonlit sky.
A new dawn is born.
A new day begins.

Spiritual awakening.
First and true vision of light.

New beginning.
Life goes on!

***

Written: 05-02-2020.

Figure 16. 'Walkies' time' with the dogs and John in our garden.

"Perfect start to a new day. Life is good."

How Do You See Yourself?

Enjoy photography and after experimenting with my digital camera this image of me was born.

So, I asked myself that same question,

"How do you see yourself?"

The result was a poem which I quickly scribbled down on a blank piece of paper, and I now share this poem with you.

Poem
I Am a Droplet in the Ocean of Time

If I exist as a droplet in the ocean of time.
Who allotted my given time on this mortal plane?

He who opened heaven's door and beckoned my spirit.
Summoned on a wave of light.

Hovered! For my time seemed immemorial.

Yet, I existed as that droplet in the ocean of time.

Time was a continued indefinite existence.
While my mind lapsed and wondered freely.

He summoned me on that wave of light.
Time-released drug soothed my mind.

Drifted into that pleasant land.
He was the watcher of my night.

Imagination, sense of time and space distorted.
As I floated across those waves of time.

Existed, as a mere droplet, in the ocean of time.

Mind but a broken timepiece!

Yesteryear's memories befuddled my mind.

Yet hope held my hand tightly.

It was not he who opened heaven's door,

Who guided me back to the shore,

From that peaceful and tranquil place.

"Remember what I said to you?
"You shall experience:
"Good days,
"Bad days,
"And very bad days."

Open, weary eyes!

Earth angel, in his white gown whispered gently,
"Welcome home."

***

Afterword:
This narrative is a dedication to my cancer team- with whom without, I would still be just:

"A Droplet in the Ocean of Time.'

***

Healers

Folklore's stories, legendary rhymes and primitive artwork show humanity has sought out alchemists, empaths, shamans, and herbalists – often referred to as 'white witches' to heal both physical and mental illnesses.

Historically all self-proclaimed 'healers' influenced the development of societies because their knowledge gave them status and power. Power that influenced rulers, leaders, kings- even you and me.

Historical tales have often hinted how even the strongest of leaders consulted their 'wise man' or local witch before going into battle.

Medical knowledge in the past was more linked to alchemy than factual medical knowledge. Herbalists and shamans were the equivalent of the local GP in such eras.

Today, medical science has surpassed itself as technological advancements finally caught up with medical discoveries.

For instance, the PET Scan is the perfect example of a medical discovery held- back, until technology caught up; to enable radiologists, scientists, and surgeons, to pin-point cancer cells more accurately- which saves and prolongs a cancer patient's lifespan.

You may ask what this knowledge has to do with 'healers' and the simple answer is: healers come in many guises.

Healers of all descriptions / guises within cultures required an inbuilt understanding of compassion. Empaths must relate to their client's needs in a spiritualistic manner gained from a mutual energy.

Love, faith, hope, and compassion defines a good healer, and we all blossom when there is someone or something to believe in.

Nevertheless, there comes a time in our lives when it may be necessary to find the courage to withstand all negative forces such as pain.

Everyone has a different threshold for pain and today- pain relief is more available to us than ever before.

Pain subdued or cancelled out; we can get on with living a more fulfilling life.

How often have we have been told to 'use it or lose it?

Well, our bodies move more freely if pain relief works, and movement is essential to our continued physical and mental well-being.

Therefore, pain relief plays an important part -not only post operatively but also throughout the recuperation period for cancer Warriors.

Recuperation Takes Time

No one can return to a normal life immediately after a serious illness or operation.

Every individual's mind and body heal at a different rate and having a 'backup' carers and   medical teams helps a person to recuperate at their own pace.

As stated before, 'time' is the one element in life which we cannot control or buy.

Therefore, we need to take time-out from our normal routines, for recuperation but that 'time-out' too can be stressful, when monetary funds are low or non-existent.

Professional, unbiased, professional advice is most helpful, especially when free and linked into your medical system; but there is too often a long 'waiting list.' Nevertheless, make yourself an appointment with them; they can be helpful.

Faith may play a significant role, in people's recovery but joining a group relevant to your needs, can give reassurance, that you are not alone fighting your illness.

A good listener is priceless – especially when they are non-judgemental and can give sensible and constructive advice.

We all must believe in our own worth and value as an individual, person.

Society itself along with our medical teams have our long-term welfare at heart, so listen to what they have to say.

Cancer will affect and impact upon your future-plans if you let it.

Accept all and any help/advice offered, when relevant to you.

Those 'bad days' seem infinite; until a friendly visitor offers you help, and my advice is: "Take it!"

Historically, traditional, alternative medicine was associated to folklore. Therefore, religious leaders, shaman, spiritual healers and so forth were the main healers in society.

Today, modern scientists and doctors tend to refer to alternative medicine as 'unproven' due to the lack of imperial scientific evidence.

Nevertheless, there are those today who still practice alternative medicine using natural remedies, herbs, and prayer.

For example, religion plays its part, when a traditional medicine Healer- applies herbs to a wound because he/she recites prayers according to their tribe's beliefs.

On the other hand, spiritual healing has no religious connection but is based on 'energy;' so, the hope for divine intervention does not apply to this branch of alternative medicine.

Worldwide revered religious sites and monuments still exist, where religious cults gather, to worship and practice their alternative beliefs.

Stonehenge

One such site is Stonehenge where Neo-Druids and New-Age groups gather periodically because they believe that nature's energy forces are within the Circle of Stonehenge -especially within Stonehenge's 'giant stones.'

As always, my narrative is a prelude to a new poem.

So just for fun, after doing a personal piece of research on Stonehenge itself, I introduce, a poem which I titled:

'Circle of Light.'

**Figure 17 Source:
http://static.pexels.com/photos/53533/stonehenge-
england-monument-stone-53533.jpeg.**

Poem
Circle of Light

Circle of Sarsen and bluestones.
'Ringing rocks.'

Place of healing,
Circle of Light.

Enduring presence.
Enticing, mystifying.

Linked to druid and King Arthur's legendary tales.
Ancient. Spiritual co-existence with man.

No blueprint.
Yet, precision built for celestial links.

Located with original intent.
By worshipers of natural forces.

Megalithic stones aliened,
To greet both summer and winter solstice.

Ritual route from life to death.
Nature's calendar for rural life.

Visiting believers' senses overwhelmed,
For they leave their intellect behind.

As they step-out of reality,
To experience its magic.

Circle of Sarsen and bluestones.
'Ringing rocks.

Place of healing?
Mystic Stonehenge, the Circle of Light,

***

Figure 18. Source:
http://static.pexels.com/photos/1448136/stonehenge-england-monument-stone-53533.jpeg.

Afterword

Let us all admit that there is something magical and mystical about Stonehenge.

Nevertheless, when one is ill or recovering from a serious disease scientifically proven medicine is essential.

Alternative medicine can prolong or cause an earlier death if used as the primary source of healing.

On the other hand, personally, I understand and respect everyone is right to choose their 'own path in life.'

"There Can Be Life After Cancer"

Figure 19. I always wear this cap when gardening in honour of my brother who died at Suez

"If you think you are the storm, cancer? Then I am the Warrior who shall defeat you!"

I, Say to You

May your: ambitions for the future be obtainable. And your dreams be friendly, restful and restore your strength.

May you: conquer your fear, and, like me, learn that there is always more to learn!

May your guardian angel walk with you, all the days of your life.

May your: notion of heaven transpires for you -here on Mother Earth.

May, we all, become better people by learning from our mistakes.

May you: accept who you were. Respect who you are now- and in the future.

"If we can achieve all these things; then we are indeed 'warriors."

My favourite poems:

One of my own favourite poems is by William Wordsworth. First recited to me when I was a child - by my father and the poem: titled: 'I wandered Lonely as a Cloud.'

I often sit in my garden on sunny days and in my mind, I see my parents sit beside me; especially when I read poetry because they enjoyed reciting their favourite poems and they were also 'good listeners.'

Always thought, that not one person's spirit lost in death if someone remembers them with love in their heart.

Parents' often have their own favourite poem, and my parents were no exception.

Sharing poetical verse, is always pleasurable.

***

Poetic Tribute to My Dad

'I Wandered Lonely as a Cloud'
By
William Wordsworth

'I wandered lonely as a cloud,
'That floats on high o'er vales and hills,
'When all at once I saw a crowd.
'A host of golden daffodils.
'Beside the lake, beneath the trees,
'Fluttering and dancing in the breeze.

'Continuous as the stars that shine,
'And twinkle on the milky way,
'They stretched in never-ending lines,
'Along the margin of the bay.
'Tossing their heads in sprightly dance.

'The waves beside them danced; but they,
'Outdid the sparkling waves in glee.
'A poet could not be gay,
'In such a jocund company.
'I gazed and gazed but little thought,
'What wealth the show to me had brought:
'For oft, when on my couch I lie,
'In a vacant or pensive mood.

'They flash upon that inward eye,
'Which is the bliss of solitude.
'And then my heart with pleasure fills,
'And danced with the daffodils.'

***

Afterword: The English language and grammar rules may have changed-over time but the sentiment of such a beautiful poem filled with imagery, does not need correcting from its original state.

This next poem is inspiring for all cancer warriors.

A poem which was my mother's personal, motivational poem.

Poem entitled: 'Happiness Ahead.'

'Happiness Ahead'

By
Patience Strong

Happiness ahead.
Yes, there is happiness ahead.
If you live believing that,
Your footsteps will be led,
In the right direction.

Though the road may twist and wind.
Walk the sunny side of life.
And you will always find,
That whatever road you tread,
There'll be happiness ahead.

***

Afterword: 'Patience Strong' was the pseudonym of Winifred Emma May. (04-06-1907 to 28-05-1990) She wrote simple, sentimental, and instrumental poems.

"Clap hands, in tribute to all cancer warriors."

For during this COVID19 Pandemic- you have all:
'Fought, the good fight, with all your might.'

'Self- isolation' has been difficult, frightening, lonely, and worrying for too many people -who have endured isolation from their 'loved-ones.'

Not everyone has survived this heart-breaking virus and many others'-are still suffering from the after-effects of COVID19's variants.

I truly wish everyone good health- whether they are Cancer Warriors' or not.

Let us all remember that not all illnesses are visible, such as PTS and depression.

***

'Stay safe, out there. Be kind to one another other."

Lady Dragon